Contents

AUTUMN!

Autumn is the season after summer, when the days get shorter, the evenings get darker, and the weather gets cooler. It can be rainy, foggy or cloudy – or bright, crisp and chilly. People go back to school and work after the summer holidays.

Nature in autumn

Plants that have been growing and flowering all summer have ripe seeds and fruit, ready for picking.

Animals like squirrels, bears and birds fill up on food before the winter comes.

Leaves turn red, golden, orange or brown, and fall off the trees ... which is why autumn is also called 'fall'.

WHAT IS AUTUMN?

Like all the seasons, autumn happens because of the way the Earth moves around the Sun.

The Earth orbits around the Sun once every year.

The Earth is tilted. As it moves around, different areas lean more towards the Sun.

When your part of the world starts to lean away from the Sun, it's autumn where you live!

Autumn

Spring

Winter

Sun

Summer

Summer

Winter

orbit

Spring

Earth

Autumn

S.T.E.A.M.

THROUGH THE SEASONS

Autumn

ANNA CLAYBOURNE

First published in Great Britain in 2019 by Wayland
Copyright © Hodder and Stoughton 2019

All rights reserved.

Senior Commissioning Editor: Melanie Palmer
Design: squareandcircus.co.uk
Illustrations: Supriya Sahai

HB ISBN 978 1 5263 0950 1
PB ISBN 978 1 5263 0951 8

Picture credits: alice photo/Shutterstock: 28b. Allia Medical
Media/Shutterstock: 16bl. aloha_17/iStockphoto: 9tl. Sawat
Banyenngam/Shutterstock: 10bl. Mircea Costina/Shutterstock:
18bl. Kobby Dagan/Shutterstock: 5t. Elena Emakova/
Shutterstock: 5c. Heartwood Films/Shutterstock: 27br. Kasom/
iStockphoto: 7cr. Michelle Lee Photography/Shutterstock: 15br.
Mr Morton/iStockphoto: 20bl. photka/Shutterstock: 9bl.
trainman111/Shutterstock: 24-5b. TRR/Shutterstock: 11b.
Nuttawut Uttamaharad/Shutterstock: 26-7c. Additional
illustrations: Freepik

Every attempt has been made to clear copyright. Should
there be any inadvertent omission please apply to the
publisher for rectification.

MIX
Paper from
responsible sources
FSC® C104740
FSC
www.fsc.org

Printed in China

Wayland
An imprint of
Hachette Children's Group
Part of Hodder and Stoughton
Carmelite House
50 Victoria Embankment
London EC4Y 0DZ

An Hachette UK Company
www.hachette.co.uk

SAFETY INFORMATION:
Please ask an adult for help with
any activities that could be tricky,
involve cooking or handling glass
or knives. Ask adult permission
when appropriate.

Due care has been taken to
ensure the activities are safe and
the publishers regret they cannot
accept liability for any loss or
injuries sustained.

Autumn festivals

Many types of crop grow through the spring and summer, and in the autumn they're ready to be harvested. People around the world hold harvest festivals, such as Chuseok in Korea, and the Moon Festival in China. In Mexico, the Day of the Dead celebrations honour those who have died with skeleton-themed costumes, sweets and bread.

Children dress up for the Day of the Dead parade in Mexico.

Lanterns are lit for the Mid-Autumn festival in Malaysia.

Autumn science

This book is full of fun science experiments, activities, and things to make in autumn.

You can do most of them with everyday craft materials and recycled objects from around the house. Turn to page 30 for some extra tips about materials and where to find them.

HAVE AN ADULT HANDY!

SOME OF THE ACTIVITIES INVOLVE SHARP OBJECTS, HEAT AND COOKING. MAKE SURE YOU ALWAYS HAVE AN ADULT TO HELP YOU, AND ASK THEM TO DO THESE PARTS.

ACORN SHOOTER

In the autumn, many plants make seeds, such as acorns, which grow on oak trees. They're fun to collect, and to shoot across the room using this catapult!

WHAT YOU NEED:

- A BOX, SUCH AS A SMALL SHOEBOX
- A PENCIL OR CHOPSTICK
- POINTED SCISSORS
- ELASTIC BANDS
- A WOODEN SPOON OR PLASTIC SERVING SPOON
- MATCHSTICKS
- STICKY TAPE
- ACORNS (OR SMALL PINE CONES, SWEETS OR PING PONG BALLS!)

Step 1:

With an adult to help, use the pointed scissors to make two holes in opposite sides of the box, near the top.

Step 2:

Fix the spoon handle to the pencil or chopstick with an elastic band, like this.

Step 3:

Push the ends of the pencil or chopstick into the holes in the box. The spoon handle needs to sit about half the way along the length of the chopstick.

Step 4:

Tie two elastic bands to the end of the spoon handle, so that they hang down, like this.

Autumn science: Seed stores

Squirrels collect acorns and other seeds, and bury them to store them for winter. They forget about some of the seeds, and they grow into new trees.

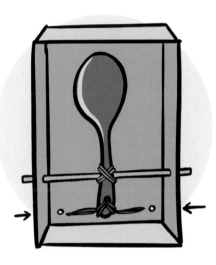

Step 5.

Make two holes in the bottom of the box, in the corners, near the spoon handle. Push the ends of the elastic bands through the holes.

Step 6.

Put matchsticks through the elastic bands, and fix them to the underside of the box with sticky tape.

Step 7.

Cut a hole in the other end of the box to make it easier to pull the spoon down. Put an acorn in the spoon, pull the spoon down, and let go!

What else can I do?

See if you can shoot acorns into a bowl or bucket.

7

PINE CONE WEATHER FORECAST

There are plenty of old stories about traditional ways to forecast the weather. They don't all work, but this one does! All you need is a pine cone.

WHAT YOU NEED:

- ONE OR MORE PINE CONES
- ONE OR MORE SMALL BOWLS
- A COVERED OUTDOOR SPACE, SUCH AS A PORCH OR COVERED BALCONY

Step 1:

Put one pine cone in each bowl. This is to stop them from rolling or blowing away when you leave them outdoors.

Step 2:

Put the bowls in a covered place outdoors, where they will be in the open air, but will not get rained on.

Step 3:

Leave the pine cones there for a few days, and check on them regularly. Do you see any changes? If the pine cones open up their scales, the pine cone forecast is for dry weather.

Autumn science:
Giving seeds a chance

A pine cone is a pine tree's version of a flower. It contains seeds that the pine tree wants to spread far and wide. When the air is getting drier, the scales open up to release their seeds, so they can blow away easily. When it's getting damper, the pine cone closes up to protect the seeds, as they won't blow away properly if they get wet.

Step 4:
If the pine cones close their scales tightly, it means rain is probably on the way.

Step 5:
Did your pine cone forecasts come true? Can you guess how it works?

What else can I make?
Most pine cones work this way, but not all. Can you find any that don't?

RAIN GAUGE

In autumn it's often rainy – and some places are rainier than others. Weather scientists measure how much rain has fallen using a rain gauge, like this one.

WHAT YOU NEED:

- A CLEAN, EMPTY, LARGE PLASTIC DRINKS BOTTLE
- STRONG STICKY TAPE
- SCISSORS
- RULER
- MARKER PEN
- OUTDOOR SPACE
- GRAVEL OR SMALL PEBBLES
- WATER

Step 1:
With an adult to help, cut off the top of the bottle, just at the point where it starts to curve in towards the neck.

Step 2:
Fill the bottom of the bottle with gravel or small pebbles, up to where the sides of the bottle are straight.

Autumn science:
How rainy?

Measuring rainfall helps scientists to figure out if the climate is getting wetter or drier over time. Thanks to climate change, some parts of the world are getting more rain, while others are becoming deserts.

Step 3:

Turn the top of the bottle upside-down and fit it inside the lower part. Fix the two parts together with strong tape.

Step 4:

Mark a line on the bottle just above the pebbles. Fill the bottle with water up to this line.

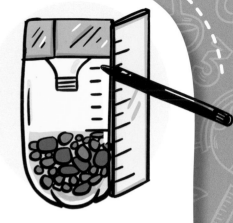

Step 5:

Use the ruler to measure upwards from the line, and mark a line every 10 mm (1 cm), or every inch, until you reach the top of the straight part of the bottle.

Step 6:

Stand the rain gauge outdoors, where it will get rained on, but will not catch drips from trees or roofs.

WATER LEVEL:
Monday 5 mm
Tuesday 5 mm
Wednesday 12 mm

Step 7:

Each day, at the same time, record how much the water level has risen. Make a chart showing the rainfall for one week.

What else can I make?

If you know someone who lives far away, ask them to make a rain gauge too, and compare your results.

ANEMOMETER

An anemometer is a machine for measuring how fast the wind is blowing. Make this simple version and test it out in some autumn winds.

WHAT YOU NEED:

- FIVE PAPER CUPS
- TWO STRAIGHT DRINKING STRAWS
- A SEWING PIN
- AN ERASER-TIPPED PENCIL
- POINTED SCISSORS
- STICKY TAPE
- GUMMED CRAFT PAPER
- A STOPWATCH OR TIMER

Step 1:
Use the scissors to make four equally spaced holes around the edge of one cup, just below the rim.

Step 2:
Push the straws through the holes in a criss-cross shape.

Step 3:
Make a hole in the bottom of the cup, and push the eraser end of the pencil through it from below.

Step 4:
Stick the pin downwards through both straws, where they cross over, and into the eraser.

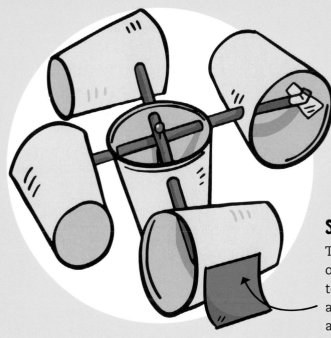

Step 5:

Make a hole in each of the other four cups, just below the rim. Push the ends of the straws into the four cups, like this.

Use tape to stick the straws to the insides of the cups to hold them in place.

Step 6:

Tape a piece of bright paper to one of the cups to make it easy to see as it spins. Hold the pencil and your anemometer should be able to spin around.

Step 7:

Hold the anemometer up in the wind, and count how many times it spins round in a minute using a stopwatch or timer.

What else can I do?

Can you blow the anemometer around as fast as the wind can?

Autumn science:
What is wind?

Wind happens when masses of air heat up and rise upwards, or cool down and sink. This makes other air rush sideways across the Earth's surface – and that's wind!

ERUPTING PUMPKIN

Pumpkins are a type of ginormous fruit that ripen in the autumn. People often hollow them out and make them into lanterns for Halloween. This pumpkin we're going to make is explosive!

WHAT YOU NEED:

- A FRESH PUMPKIN
- AN ICE CREAM SCOOP
- A SHARP KNIFE
- BICARBONATE OF SODA (BAKING SODA)
- FOOD COLOURING (OPTIONAL)
- A TABLESPOON
- WHITE VINEGAR
- AN OUTDOOR SPACE, OR LOTS OF NEWSPAPER!

Step 1:

Ask an adult to cut the top off the pumpkin, scoop out the insides with the ice cream scoop, and carve a face. You should give the pumpkin a large mouth, near the bottom.

Step 2:

Put about three tablespoons of bicarbonate of soda (baking soda) into the bottom of the pumpkin, and add a little food colouring (green or red look good).

Step 3:

Take the pumpkin outdoors, or spread out a thick layer of newspaper for it to sit on.

Step 4:

Working quickly, pour three tablespoons of vinegar into the pumpkin to make it erupt!

Autumn science:
Explosive reactions

When vinegar and bicarbonate of soda mix together, there's an instant chemical reaction. Both chemicals change and create new chemicals. One of these is carbon dioxide gas. As more and more bubbles of gas form, the mixture foams up and splurges out of the pumpkin's mouth.

Fizz!

Vinegar + Bicarbonate of Soda = bubbles!

What else can I do?

Ask an adult to warm the vinegar up in a microwave before you use it. Does it work better?

SPOOKY HAND

Celebrate spooky autumn festivals such as Halloween or the Day of the Dead with a scary working hand!

WHAT YOU NEED:

- STIFF CARD
- PENCIL
- SCISSORS
- BENDY DRINKING STRAWS
- STICKY TAPE
- STRING
- FELT-TIP PENS
- AN ADULT TO HELP
- MEASURING TAPE OR RULER

Step 1:
Draw around an adult's hand on to the card. Make sure you include some of the wrist, like this.

Step 2:
Carefully cut the hand out. Check on the real hand where the fingers and thumb bend, and mark bending lines on the card hand.

Autumn science:
Stringy fingers

When you pull on the strings, they get shorter, and make the fingers bend inwards. It's not just your model hand that works this way – real hands do too! Fingers have tough strings called tendons connected to them. Muscles in your arms pull on the tendons to make your fingers bend.

Muscles

Tendons

Step 3:

Use tape to stick a straw to each finger, making the bendy parts all line up at the wrist, and trim off the ends. Only put tape in between the bending lines.

Tape down string at tips

Tape only between bendy lines

Bendy parts should line up

String through each straw

Step 4:

At the bending lines, carefully snip tiny triangle shapes out of the upper side of each straw, like this.

Step 5:

Cut five pieces of string, each about 30 cm long. Thread one piece of string through each finger and stick it in place at the tip.

Step 6:

To make it work, hold the hand by the wrist, and pull on the strings.

Turn your hand over and colour in the other side, making it look as spooky as possible!

What else can I do?

Grip one of your arms firmly, just above your wrist, and wiggle your fingers. Can you feel the tendons working?

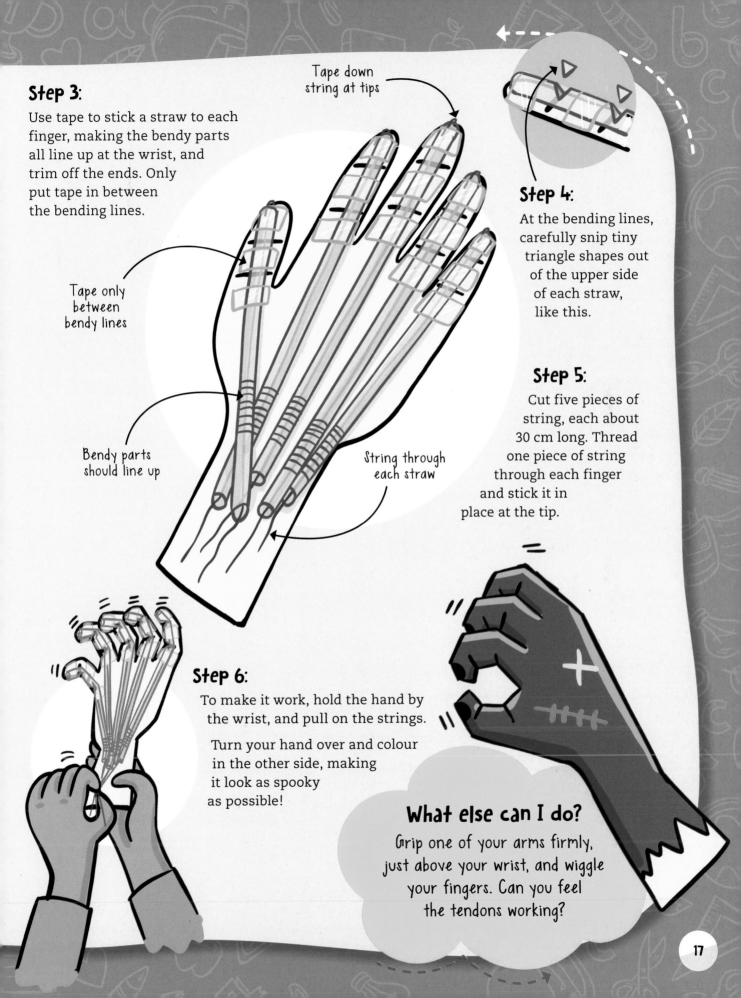

MAKE A SPIDER WEB

In autumn, you sometimes see spider webs weighed down with gleaming raindrops. This giant, but realistic, spider web makes a great decoration for a bedroom or a party.

WHAT YOU NEED:

- A BALL OF WHITE, PALE GREY, SILVER OR SPARKLY KNITTING YARN
- DRAWING PINS OR THUMBTACKS
- SCISSORS
- A CORNER OF A ROOM WHERE YOU CAN PUT YOUR SPIDER WEB

Step 1:

Ask an adult's permission before you start.

First, with an adult to help, stick the pins or tacks into the wall in a large triangle across a corner, like this.

Autumn science:
Spidery skills

This is how real spiders make their webs. They don't have to learn to do it – it's an instinct, a behaviour that is built into them. They use spider silk, which they spin from glands in their abdomens. It's very strong, and can support a lot of weight, such as heavy raindrops.

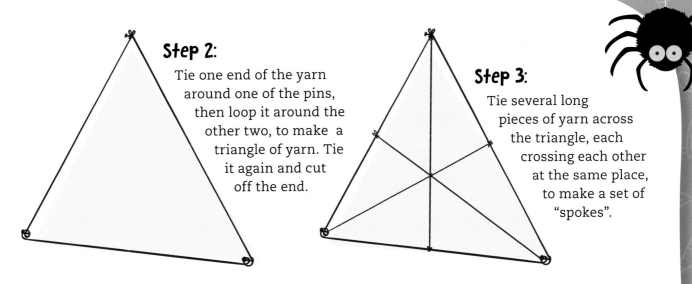

Step 2:

Tie one end of the yarn around one of the pins, then loop it around the other two, to make a triangle of yarn. Tie it again and cut off the end.

Step 3:

Tie several long pieces of yarn across the triangle, each crossing each other at the same place, to make a set of "spokes".

Step 4:

Now start with a new piece of yarn, and tie it to the middle. Work outwards in a spiral, looping the yarn around each of the spokes in turn.

Step 5:

When your piece of yarn runs out, just tie on a new piece. Keep going until you reach the triangle around the edge, then tie the yarn and snip off any loose ends.

What else can I make?

- Tie or glue clear beads to the web to make raindrops.
- Can you make a spider to put in the middle too?

MYSTERIOUS SLIME

You've probably made slime before – but this slime is special. It behaves in some very strange ways. Try it as an indoor or party activity.

WHAT YOU NEED:

- A PACKET OF CORNFLOUR (CORNSTARCH)
- A CUP OF WATER
- GREEN FOOD COLOURING (OPTIONAL)
- A LARGE MIXING BOWL
- A LARGE WOODEN SPOON

Step 1:
Pour the water into the bowl, and add a few drops of food colouring.

FARE! Kviksand
DANGER! Quicksand
ACHTUNG! Quicksand

Autumn science: Oobleck!

This strange substance is sometimes called oobleck. It's very unusual because it turns solid under pressure, but can also flow like a liquid. Quicksand works a bit like this too. That's why you can sink into it, but it's hard to get out.

Step 2:

Add the cornflour bit by bit, stirring the mixture with the spoon until you have runny, gloopy slime. (You'll probably need almost twice as much cornflour as water.)

Step 3:

If it's hard to stir the slime, try moving the spoon more slowly. The slower you stir, the runnier the slime is!

Step 5:

See if you can grab some slime and squeeze it tightly into a solid ball. Then open your hand out. What happens?

Step 4:

Try hitting the slime hard with the spoon or your fist. Then try pressing it gently. What happens?

What else can I make?

Try a slime quicksand experiment. Put some slime in a small, flat-bottomed food container, and stand a plastic toy figure in it. Try pulling the figure out very quickly - then try slowly. What happens?

HEAR LIKE A BAT

In autumn, you sometimes see bats at dusk, feeding on insects before hibernating in winter. Bats hunt by making sounds, and listening for echoes that bounce off prey. Try doing this yourself!

WHAT YOU NEED:

- A CLEAN, DRY FOIL FOOD CONTAINER
- A CARDBOARD TUBE, LIKE THE TUBE FROM A ROLL OF KITCHEN PAPER
- ANOTHER PERSON TO HELP
- A BLINDFOLD

Step 1:

Open out the foil container and flatten the edges, to make a curved dish shape. Give it to the other person to hold.

Autumn science: Bat senses

The way bats sense prey is called echolocation. Some whales and dolphins do it too. Using echoes, they can work out where things are, and catch them easily.

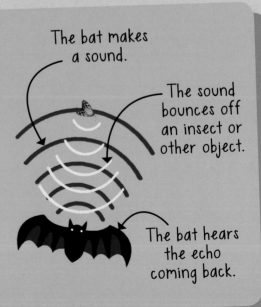

The bat makes a sound.

The sound bounces off an insect or other object.

The bat hears the echo coming back.

Step 2:

Put on the blindfold and make sure you can't see anything. Hold the cardboard tube up to your mouth.

Step 3:

Practise making sharp, loud sounds through the tube. Try clicking your tongue, or doing short, high-pitched squeaks.

Step 4:

As you do this, ask the other person to slowly move the foil container past the end of the tube, making sure it doesn't touch it.

Step 5:

Can you tell when the foil container is right in front of you? If you listen carefully, you should be able to hear a slight metallic echo as it passes by.

What else can I do?

Look out for bats when it's getting dark outdoors. They fly in a swooping, fluttering motion, near trees and buildings.

EXPLODING CORN

Maize, or corn, is one of many farm crops that ripen and are harvested in autumn. Popcorn is made using dried kernels of corn.

WHAT YOU NEED:
- A PACK OF POPPING CORN
- A MICROWAVE
- A BROWN PAPER BAG
- SUGAR OR SALT (OPTIONAL)

Step 1:
Open the paper bag and check it has no holes, or metal parts such as staples. Put a handful of popping corn into the bag.

Autumn science:
Heat explosion

Popcorn kernels contain some water. As it heats up in the microwave, this water boils and makes steam. But popcorn kernels have a tough, hard skin. The steam pushes against the skin, until the kernel explodes and POPS.

Step 2:
Fold the top over tightly three times, so that it stays closed.

24

Step 3:

Put the bag into the microwave, and heat on full power for about 2 minutes, with an adult to supervise.

POP!!

Step 4:

After a while, you should hear the corn popping. When the popping sound slows down or stops, turn the microwave off.

Yum!

Step 5:

Ask an adult to carefully take out the bag and open it (some hot steam will come out). Eat the popped corn as it is, or sprinkle with a little sugar or salt first.

What else can I do?

With an adult to help, put a marshmallow on a microwaveable plate, and microwave it on full power for about 10 seconds. It won't explode, but it will grow! Can you figure out why?

STARGAZING

In autumn, the nights get darker earlier, but it's still not too cold ... perfect for stargazing!

WHAT YOU NEED:

- A CLEAR, DARK NIGHT
- WARM CLOTHES
- A PICNIC BLANKET
- A TORCH
- A SAFE OUTDOOR SPACE, WITH GRASS TO LIE ON
- AN ADULT TO GO WITH YOU
- BINOCULARS OR A TELESCOPE, IF YOU HAVE ANY

Autumn science:
Eyes for the skies

When it's very dark, the pupils in your eyes open wide to let in as much light as possible. It takes a few minutes until you can see the stars really clearly. But if there are bright lights nearby, your pupils will stay smaller.

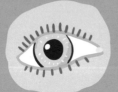

In the dark

In brightness

Northern Hemisphere

Cygnus, the swan

Orion, the huntsman

Cassiopeia, the beautiful queen

The plough or big dipper

Pegasus, the flying horse

Southern Hemisphere

Crux,
the Southern Cross

Monoceros, the
unicorn

Volans,
the flying
fish

Canis Major,
the large dog

Puppis, the
poop deck

The Milky Way

Step 1:
Use the torch to find your way safely to a good stargazing spot. It should be away from bright streetlights or house lights.

Step 2:
If you're stargazing in the garden, turn off the lights in the house, to make it as dark as possible.

Step 3:
Spread out the picnic rug and lie on it, looking up at the sky. Turn the torch off and wait at least five minutes for your eyes to adjust to the darkness.

Step 4:
Look for interesting stars and constellations (star patterns). Here are some constellations to spot in the northern and southern hemispheres.

Step 5:
You may also be able to see the Milky Way, a thick streak of stars across the sky. This is the view into the thickest part of our galaxy.

What else can I do?

As well as constellations, look out for "shooting stars". They are not actually stars, but bits of dust or rock falling into the Earth's atmosphere. They burn up, making a bright streak across the sky.

LEAF FOSSILS

Most fossils are of hard animal parts, like skeletons and seashells. But there are some leaf fossils, too. You can use fallen autumn leaves to make your own leaf "fossils".

WHAT YOU NEED:

- CLEAN, DRY FALLEN LEAVES
- AIR-DRYING CLAY
- GREASEPROOF PAPER
- ROLLING PIN
- CLEAR VARNISH OR PAINT (OPTIONAL)

Step 1:

Take a piece of clay about the size of your fist, and roll it into a ball. Put it on a table between two pieces of greaseproof paper.

Autumn science:
Falling and forming

Most fossils form when living things are covered in layers of mud, which hardens into stone. This often happens at the bottom of seas or lakes, where mud constantly collects. So a leaf fossil might have formed when a leaf fell off a tree into water, and sank to the bottom.

Step 2:

Roll the clay into a flat circle, between the pieces of paper. This makes sure it has no fingerprints on it.

Step 3:

Gently press a leaf onto the clay, underside down. Press it all over so that all the leaf veins are pushed into the clay.

Step 4:

Carefully peel the leaf off, starting at the stalk. If any bits of leaf are left behind, lift them off using a pin.

Step 5:

Let the clay dry completely. If you like, you can varnish it, or paint it to look like stone.

What else can I do?

Make a mini leaf fossil with a small leaf, and make a hole in the clay with a skewer before it dries. Then you can hang it on a string or use it to make a necklace.

MATERIALS

This list shows you where to find the materials you need for the activities in this book.

FROM A CRAFT OR HOBBY SHOP:
- KNITTING YARN
- AIR-DRYING CLAY
- CLEAR VARNISH
- PAINT

BASIC ART AND CRAFT MATERIALS:
- STICKY TAPE
- RULER
- MARKER PENS
- FELT-TIP PENS • PENCILS
- PAPER • CARD
- SCISSORS
- GLUE
- STRING

FROM A SUPERMARKET OR GARDEN CENTRE:
- PUMPKIN
- POPPING CORN
- GRAVEL
- PAPER CUPS
- BENDY STRAWS
- FOIL FOOD CONTAINERS
- BROWN PAPER BAGS

FROM THE KITCHEN:
- MICROWAVE
- CHOPSTICKS • SHARP KNIFE
- WOODEN SPOONS
- SERVING SPOONS • ROLLING PIN
- MATCHSTICKS • FOOD COLOURING
- GLASSES, BOWLS, JUGS, CUPS, PLATES AND SAUCERS
- PLASTIC BOTTLES • WHITE VINEGAR
- WATER • SUGAR • SALT
- ICE CREAM SCOOP
- CARDBOARD KITCHEN ROLL TUBE
- BICARBONATE OF SODA (BAKING SODA)
- CORNFLOUR (CORNSTARCH)
- GREASEPROOF PAPER

FROM AROUND THE HOUSE:
- BOXES • SEWING PINS
- ELASTIC BANDS • TORCH
- STOPWATCH OR TIMER
- DRAWING PINS OR THUMBTACKS
- BLINDFOLD (SUCH AS A SCARF)
- PICNIC BLANKET
- BINOCULARS OR TELESCOPE

FROM A PARK:
- ACORNS
- PINE CONES • PEBBLES
- FALLEN LEAVES

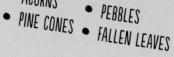
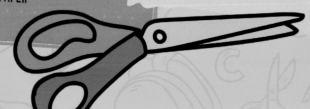

Glossary

abdomen The main part of an animal's body, where its stomach is.

anemometer A machine for measuring wind speed.

atmosphere The layer of gases surrounding the Earth.

carbon dioxide A type of gas that is found in the air, and forms in some chemical reactions.

chemical reaction A process that makes some substances change when they mix together.

climate The typical weather conditions in a particular place or area.

climate change A change in climate patterns around the world.

constellation A group of stars that appear to form a pattern.

crops Plants grown on farms as a food supply.

echo A sound that has reflected off a surface.

echolocation Sensing surroundings by making sounds and listening for the echoes that bounce off surfaces.

fall Another name for autumn.

fossil The remains or trace of a prehistoric living thing, preserved in rock.

galaxy A huge cluster or spiral of stars in space.

gauge An instrument for measuring something.

gland A type of body organ that makes a useful substance.

harvest To pick and gather crops when they are ready to use.

hibernate To spend the winter in a sleep-like state.

instinct A type of animal behaviour that is automatic or built-in, and does not have to be learned.

Northern Hemisphere The half of the Earth north of the equator, including the North Pole.

orbit To circle around another object, such as a planet orbiting around the Sun.

prey An animal that is hunted and eaten by another animal.

pupil The round, dark circle in the centre of an eye that lets light into the eye.

quicksand A type of wet sand that is easy to sink into.

shooting star A streak of light across the night sky, caused by rock burning up in the Earth's atmosphere.

Southern Hemisphere The half of the Earth south of the equator, including the South Pole.

tendons String-like body parts that connect muscles to bones, and pull on bones to make them move.

Index